Not What You Meant

Not What You Meant

...and why AI keeps
answering anyway

Andres Velasquez

ISBN: 979-8-9944223-0-4 (Paperback)

Published in Orlando, Florida.

Library of Congress Control Number: 2025928257

Book design by Andres Velasquez.

First printing edition 2026.

NotWhatYouMeant.com

To my family.

Table of contents

Introduction

I kept having the same quiet argument with my computer.

Not a dramatic one. Just that low-grade frustration where you stare at the screen thinking, there is no way this thing and I are working on the same problem.

I'd ask for something reasonable. An explanation. A draft. Help thinking through a decision. The response would come back confident, articulate... and somehow useless.

So I'd try again. Add a sentence. Clarify a bit. Tighten the wording.

Sometimes that worked. Sometimes it didn't. And that inconsistency was the part that bothered me. Same tool. Same person. Completely different outcomes. No obvious reason.

The explanation everyone seems to settle on is that AI — the systems generating these responses — is unreliable. Not quite ready. Impressive in demos, frustrating in real work. Maybe in a few years it'll get better.

I believed that for a while. Mostly because it was the easiest explanation available.

What took me longer than it should have to notice was how often I assumed the machine knew what I meant. How much context I carried in my head and never actually said. How many decisions I left unstated because, to me, they felt obvious.

After the fifth or sixth time I caught myself thinking WTF, it stopped being a reaction and started feeling like the universe was messing with me.

Same letters. Same moment. Over and over.

Eventually I realized it wasn't a coincidence. It was a pattern I hadn't been paying attention to.

What am I actually asking for?
Who is this for, really?
What would a usable answer even look like?

Once I started paying attention to those questions, the results stopped feeling random. Not perfect—but predictable.

Around the same time, something else clicked that made all of this feel uncomfortably familiar.

I'm bad at reading between the lines.

Tone, hints, implied meaning—if it isn't said out loud, there's a good chance I'll miss it. This has been true for most of my life. It's especially true at home, where I've learned (repeatedly) that there are entire conversations happening that I'm not aware I'm participating in.

What other people seem to pick up intuitively, I usually need spelled out. Not because I don't care—but because I don't infer well.

Which is probably why working with AI felt less alien than it does to most people.

AI behaves similarly. It doesn't read tone. It doesn't detect what you probably meant. If something isn't stated, it fills in the blanks with whatever seems most reasonable—and moves on.

For most of our lives, that hasn't been a problem. People ask follow-up questions. They adjust. They give us the benefit of the doubt. A lot of work gets done on shared context alone.

AI doesn't do that on its own.

When something is missing, it doesn't pause. It doesn't ask. It just assumes. Confidently.

That's where the surprise usually comes from. Not because AI is broken—but because the shortcuts most of us have relied on forever suddenly stop working.

That realization also explains something else I keep hearing in conversations.

The tension. The half-jokes. The defensiveness. The way otherwise smart, capable people talk about AI, like it is either magic or a threat.

It isn't about tools. It is about what those tools are quietly changing.

At some point, most conversations about AI run into the same quiet fear: Is this going to replace me?

What I started noticing is that, in most contexts, AI doesn't replace people. It disrupts the habit of leaving things unsaid and expecting the other side to fill in the gaps correctly.

This isn't about personal growth.

It's about what happens when being clear stops being optional.

This is not a book about clever phrasing or prompt tricks. It's not a collection of templates, and it's not about getting a model to sound smarter.

It's about noticing what you leave unstated when you ask for work to be done—and what changes when you stop doing that.

You catch yourself before hitting send. You notice missing pieces earlier.

Not efficiency.
Not productivity.

Just this: can the other side actually work with what I gave them?

When they can't, machines guess.

Most of what follows starts there.

ACT I

1

Seeing The Problem Clearly

Before tools, techniques, or frameworks can help, something more basic has to happen: you have to see the problem for what it actually is. Not as a failure. Not as a lack of skill. Not as a technology that isn't ready yet.

But as a shift in how work moves from intention to execution.

The chapters that follow are about noticing where things start to drift—often quietly, often without anyone doing anything "wrong." They're about understanding why approaches that worked for years suddenly feel unreliable, and why that change isn't temporary.

Nothing in this section requires you to do anything differently yet.

There's no action to take. No behavior to adopt.

Just a clearer picture of what changed, where assumptions stopped holding, and why guessing—by people or machines—no longer produces the results it used to.

2

The Gap

By the time something goes wrong with AI, it usually looks fine.

Not obviously wrong. Not broken. Just... slightly off.

The output makes sense. It follows instructions. It sounds confident. If you're skimming, it even looks done.

The problem only shows up later—when that output has to be used for something real. When it meets a situation it wasn't shaped for.

That's why these failures are hard to pin down. Nothing clearly fails in the moment. There's no error message to point to. Just a growing sense that the result doesn't quite fit the situation it was meant for.

That's when the gap becomes visible.

Not because something failed loudly, but because something important was never accounted for in the first place.

An email that technically answers the question but creates more confusion.
A summary that includes all the points but misses the point.
A plan that looks solid until it actually has to be executed.

Nothing here feels dramatic. That's part of the problem.

When things fail this way, it's easy to blame execution. Or timing. Or the tool itself. It's much harder to notice that the instruction — what you explicitly told the system to do — may never have been complete to begin with.

What usually goes missing isn't intelligence.

It's intent.

Not the overall goal—that part is often clear. What's missing are the details you assumed didn't need to be said. The ones that felt obvious at the time.

When something is left out, the model — the system producing the response — doesn't hesitate. It commits to an interpretation and moves on. From the outside, the result looks confident. From the inside, it's solving a slightly different problem than the one you had in mind.

That's why these breakdowns are so frustrating.

There's no single moment where you can point and say, that's where it went wrong. Everything looks defensible. Nothing looks broken.

Until you start looking for the gap.

It becomes visible—not just with AI, but anywhere work moves from intention to execution.

3

What Changed

For most of our working lives, being vague has been fine.

Not ideal, maybe. But workable.

You could start a sentence and trust the other person to land where you were heading. You could outline the general shape of something and expect the details to get worked out along the way. You could say "make this better" and the person on the other end would figure out what better meant in context.

That wasn't lazy. It was normal.

Human communication runs on inference — filling in meaning that wasn't explicitly stated. We read tone. We notice hesitation. We fill in gaps based on everything else we know about the situation.

And when that breaks down, there's a repair mechanism built in.

Someone asks a question. Someone pauses. Someone gives you a look that makes it very clear they didn't understand what you meant.

Sometimes you fix it. Sometimes you realize you missed something that was obvious to everyone else. Either way, the conversation doesn't just move on pretending everything is fine.

That's what made ambiguity — instructions that leave room for interpretation — safe.

It wasn't that instructions were always clear. It's that they didn't have to be. The gaps got closed in real time by people who understood the context, cared about the outcome, and could tell when something didn't make sense.

In other cases, people like me were left wondering what just happened—but that's a different problem.

That environment doesn't exist everywhere anymore.

Not because people stopped being helpful. But because a lot of work now moves through systems that don't interpret the way humans do.

When a detail is left unstated, nothing asks about it. Nothing hesitates. The instruction goes in. And whatever was unclear goes with it.

Not that being vague is suddenly wrong. It's that being vague used to be a rough draft, and now it's a final instruction.

The environment absorbed ambiguity before. Now it reflects it back.

4

Demystification Without Instruction

The first few times AI gave me a confident answer that turned out to be wrong, I assumed it was hallucinating — the term people use when a system confidently makes something up.

That word gets used a lot. It sounds dramatic. Like the model broke character, invented something, went rogue.

What took me longer to notice was that the confidence level never changed.

Right answers sounded confident. Wrong answers sounded confident. Partial answers that missed the entire point sounded confident. The tone stayed consistent regardless of whether the content held up.

That's not hallucination. That's just how the thing talks.

AI doesn't evaluate whether something is true before producing an answer. It completes patterns — continuing text in whatever way statistically fits best. If the pattern it's completing leads somewhere reasonable-sounding, it follows that path. If it leads somewhere wrong, it still follows it—with the same steady tone.

There's no internal warning system. No hesitation when certainty drops. The output reads the same whether it's reciting something well-established or stitching together something plausible from fragments.

That consistency is what makes the errors so disorienting.

When a person is unsure, you can usually tell. They hedge. They slow down. They say "I think" or "probably" or "let me double-check that." The uncertainty leaks through.

AI doesn't leak intent.

It generates sentences that flow well. It uses transitions that sound logical. It maintains a tone that suggests everything is on solid ground—even when it isn't.

That fluency — how smooth and readable the output sounds — is a feature, not a sign of understanding.

It's optimized to sound coherent. To feel readable. To move from one sentence to the next without friction. And it does that extremely well.

But fluency and accuracy are separate things. One doesn't guarantee the other.

What makes this tricky is that most of the time, fluency is enough. If something reads well and seems plausible, we tend to move forward with it. We don't stop to verify every claim or trace every assumption back to its source. (Think of politicians or car sellers, hard to separate good from bad just from their speeches).

That works fine when the person on the other end has some idea of what they're talking about. It doesn't work as well when the output is just pattern completion —filling in what usually comes next based on what it's seen before— wearing a confident voice.

The other piece that confused me early on was how often the answers were almost right.

Not completely off. Not nonsense. Just missing a detail. Or framed slightly wrong. Or technically accurate but useless in context.

That near-miss quality made it harder to pin down what was happening. If something is fully wrong, you notice. If it's mostly right, you assume the rest is solid too. (As humans, we tend to assume if something is mostly wrong it is fully wrong. The other way works too, if it is mostly right, it's completely right)

What I eventually realized is that AI doesn't distinguish between those states. It's not aiming for mostly right. It's completing the instruction as given, using whatever patterns fit.

If the instruction leaves room for interpretation — meaning it can be understood in more than one way— the model interprets. If a detail is unstated, the model fills it in. If the context is ambiguous, the model picks a version and runs with it.

None of that involves checking whether the choice it made was the one you had in mind.

It follows instructions. It completes patterns. It produces output that sounds like language because it is language—arranged in ways that statistically make sense based on what it's seen before.

What it doesn't do is pause and think, wait, is this actually what they meant?

Once I stopped expecting that pause, the behavior stopped feeling random.

Not perfect. Not foolproof. But predictable.

If the instruction is clear, the output tends to be useful. If the instruction has gaps, the output reflects those gaps—confidently.

The confidence doesn't mean the answer is right. It just means the model finished the task it thought it was given.

That distinction matters more than it seems, like it should.

5

What's Usually Missing

The frustrating part isn't that something goes wrong.

It's that when you go back to look at what you asked for, there's nothing obviously wrong with the request.

The phrasing is fine. The task is clear. You said what you wanted.

And yet.

What I started noticing—after enough rounds of this—was that the problem wasn't usually in what I said. It was in what I didn't say because it felt too obvious to mention.

Most of us do this without thinking about it.

We describe what we want made, but not what it's supposed to do once it exists. We ask for an explanation, but don't mention who needs to understand it. We ask for an update, but leave out whether it's meant to inform, persuade, or help someone decide.

None of that feels like missing information. It feels like context that should be clear from the situation.

Except the situation isn't clear to the system receiving the instruction.

It doesn't know what happens next. It doesn't know who this is for. It doesn't know what you're trying to prioritize or work around.

So it guesses.

And the guess is usually reasonable. It's just not the one you were expecting.

That gap—between what feels obvious to you and what actually got communicated—shows up in the same places again and again.

Sometimes it shows up in what the output is supposed to do once it's finished.

A draft email might be meant to clear up confusion, calm someone down, or buy time. Same task. Very different choices about tone, length, and what gets emphasized.

If that difference isn't mentioned, the result can be technically correct but feel wrong for the situation. Or the right tone applied to the wrong moment.

Other times, it shows up in who the output is for.

In normal conversation, we adjust for this automatically. We notice confusion. We slow down. We change how we're explaining things as we go.

That doesn't happen here.

There are also limits that never get said out loud.

The quiet rules that shape what's acceptable and what isn't. How long is too long. How formal is too formal. What can be said directly, and what needs to be handled carefully.

These aren't rules you usually write down. They're just part of how things work in a given situation.

But when they aren't stated, they don't exist.

The result might be too casual for the context. Or too long for the format. Or miss that certain things can't be said directly, even if they're true.

What took me longer to notice is how often success itself is left undefined.

Not the task. The task is usually clear. But what it means for the output to actually work.

Sometimes "work" just means the answer is correct. Sometimes it means it helps someone make a decision.
Sometimes it means it saves the next person time instead of creating more questions.

If that part stays unstated, the result can check all the obvious boxes and still not be usable.

I ran into this constantly with anything that involved a decision.

I'd get back something that laid out options clearly, explained the trade-offs, and pointed out the risks. And I'd sit there thinking, okay... but which one do we pick?

What was missing wasn't information. It was what mattered more in that moment.

Speed or accuracy?
Playing it safe or trying something new?

Those aren't questions the system can answer. And when they're not addressed, the output stays neutral. Helpful, but non-committal.

None of this is dramatic.

Each gap on its own is small. Fixable. The kind of thing you can patch in a follow-up.

But what I started noticing is how consistent the pattern was.

It wasn't random. It wasn't unpredictable.

It was the same few things, showing up over and over, in slightly different forms.

They start feeling like the thing you should have been noticing all along.

6

The Same Shape

After the third or fourth time something lands wrong, you start looking for a pattern.

Not because you're trying to solve it yet. Just because randomness is exhausting, and patterns at least make things predictable.

What I noticed first was how similar the failures looked.

Not the details. Those were always different. But the shape of what went wrong felt consistent.

A document that checked every requirement but didn't help anyone decide what to do next.
A meeting agenda that looked thorough but led to an hour of circular discussion.
A request that was clear about the task but left the person executing it guessing what actually mattered.

Different situations. Different tasks. Same underlying problem.

Something that should have been obvious—wasn't said.

That repetition is what made me start paying closer attention to what was actually happening.

When I went back through requests that didn't land right, the missing piece was never the same thing twice. Sometimes it was who the output was for. Sometimes it was what it needed to do once it existed. Sometimes it was a constraint that felt too basic to mention.

But the structure of the mistake was identical every time.

The instruction described what to make.
It didn't describe what making it well actually required.

That gap showed up everywhere. Not just with AI. Anywhere work moved from one person to another without the full picture traveling with it.

Once I started watching for it, I saw it constantly.

In handoffs that looked complete but left the next person guessing.
In explanations that covered the topic but didn't help anyone decide what to do.
In requests that were clear about the task but vague about everything else that mattered.

The problem wasn't that people were being careless. Most of the time, the missing parts didn't need to be said. They got filled in naturally by whoever was on the receiving end.

Until they didn't.

What made this harder to spot was that nothing looked broken in the instruction itself.

The phrasing was fine. The task was clear. You could read it back and not see anything obviously wrong.

The issue only became visible when the output had to meet reality—and reality cared about things the instruction never mentioned.

That's when it clicked.

These weren't separate problems.

They were the same problem, showing up in different ways.

The shape was always the same: something essential was assumed to be obvious and never made explicit.

What changed was which essential thing got left out.

Sometimes it was the outcome the work was supposed to create. Sometimes it was the person who needed to understand it. Sometimes it was the rules that shaped what was acceptable and what wasn't.

But the reason things kept landing wrong was identical.

The instruction treated context like it would follow along on its own.

And it didn't.

I kept noticing this. Not in a structured way. Just seeing the same shape in situations that looked completely different on the surface.

At some point, it stopped feeling like a collection of issues and started feeling like one thing I didn't have a name for yet.

Not because I'd figured out how to fix it.

But because I could finally see what actually needed to be fixed.

7

Naming the Shape

The failures we've been looking at weren't random, and they weren't subtle. They followed the same structure every time.

The instruction described what needed to be made. What it left out was what making it well actually required.

Sometimes the instruction left out what the work was supposed to accomplish once it existed. Sometimes it left out who it was for. And sometimes it never defined what a usable result actually looked like.

Different omissions. Same outcome.

Without those boundaries, the result could still miss the mark.

Those three pieces—what the work is supposed to do, who it's for, and what a usable result needs to look like—turned out to be the shape I kept seeing.

Not separately. Together.

When one was missing, things drifted. When two were missing, the output became a guess. When all three were missing, the instruction might as well have been a rough draft someone assumed would get clarified later.

At some point, I needed a way to refer to this without explaining it every time.

The three pieces already had names that worked well enough:

WHAT — what the output is supposed to accomplish

TARGET — who or what it's for

FORMAT — what a usable result needs to look like

Together, that's WTF.

Not the reaction. The structure.

Every miss that showed up earlier in the book fits here.

When the purpose was unclear, the output drifted. When the audience wasn't specified, it aimed nowhere in particular.
When the shape of a usable result wasn't defined, it guessed.

Different failures. Same gaps.

This isn't a trick. It's not phrasing advice. It's not about sounding clever or finding the right words.

It's just a way of seeing what tends to be missing when work moves from intention to execution. A lens that makes the gaps easier to spot before they turn into problems.

It doesn't solve anything on its own. But once the shape has a name, it becomes easier to notice when something is missing—and harder to assume it will get filled in later.

Now that it has a name.

ACT II

8

Why This Stopped Being Optional

By now, the pattern should be familiar.

Not in a technical sense. In a lived one.

You've seen how work can look correct and still fail. How instructions that feel clear produce results that don't quite fit. How nothing appears broken in the moment, and yet something important never lands.

Act I wasn't about fixing that.

It was about noticing it.

What Act II is about is why that same pattern suddenly carries consequences it didn't used to.

The gaps we've been talking about aren't new. Work has always moved forward on incomplete instructions. Context has always lived in people's heads. Assumptions have always filled in the space between what was said and what was meant.

For a long time, that worked.

Not because instructions were complete. But because the environment repaired what was missing.

People asked follow-up questions. They inferred intent. They adjusted based on shared understanding of what mattered and what didn't. Ambiguity was survivable because someone downstream absorbed it.

That environment is less reliable now.

Not because people got worse at their jobs. And not because tools are suddenly fragile.

Because more work now moves through systems that don't pause to interpret. They don't ask clarifying questions. They don't notice when something feels off. They execute what they're given and move on.

What used to get fixed later now just moves forward.

That shift doesn't announce itself. Nothing feels dramatically different when you're writing a request or handing something off. The work still gets done. Outputs still come back. Most of the time, things look fine.

The difference only shows up when the result has to meet reality.

That's when it becomes clear that something you assumed would get filled in never was.

Act II isn't about learning a new way to work.

It's about understanding why a way of working that used to be safe quietly stopped being so.

Why gaps that were once tolerable now propagate. Why "good enough" instructions now produce brittle results. Why clarity moved from being helpful to being structural.

The chapters that follow don't introduce a method.

They name a shape that's been there the whole time.

Just to make it clear why doing nothing different no longer produces the same outcomes it used to.

9

What Specification Actually Is

None of this is new.

That part needs to be clear from the start.

When work moves from one person to another, it carries instructions—sometimes formal, sometimes not. A brief. A ticket. A request. A note on what needs to happen next.

Those instructions have always needed to be clear enough for the other person to do something useful with them.

That requirement didn't suddenly appear because AI exists.

What did appear was a situation where being unclear stopped working the way it used to.

Before, when something was ambiguous, there was room to fix it. Someone could ask a question. Someone could push back. Someone could say, "wait, what do you actually need here?"

That loop closed gaps in real time.

Now, more of those handoffs happen through systems that don't ask questions. The instruction goes in. Whatever was unclear stays unclear. The work proceeds anyway.

Not that being clear became important.

It's that being unclear stopped being recoverable.

If you look at how specifications have always functioned—design briefs, project tickets, requirements docs—the structure underneath is consistent.

The person receiving the work needs to know what the output is supposed to accomplish once it's done. They need to know who or what it's for. And they need to know what a finished result should actually look like.

When those pieces are present.

When they're not, someone has to guess. And when the person guessing knows the context, that usually works out. They fill in what was missing based on everything else they understand about the situation.

But when they don't—or when there isn't a person on the other end at all—the guess becomes final.

That's where the discomfort lives.

Not in learning something new. In realizing that something you thought was clear enough actually wasn't. And the environment that used to absorb that ambiguity isn't there anymore.

Most professionals already tighten handoffs when the cost of being misunderstood is high.

More detail. Clearer boundaries. Less left to interpretation.

Not because the task is harder.

Because the mistake is more expensive.

What changed is that the cost threshold moved.

Ambiguity that used to be low-cost—because it got resolved through follow-up or shared understanding—is now higher-cost.

Because it doesn't get resolved.

It gets executed.

This isn't about prompts. Or phrasing. Or finding the right words to make a machine do what you want.

It's about specifying work clearly enough that it can be done without a human filling in the gaps.

What didn't exist was the need to use it every time.

The lens that got named in the last chapter—WHAT, TARGET, FORMAT—isn't a new way of thinking about work.

It's a way of naming what was already there, so it's easier to notice when something's missing.

None of that is prompting.

It's just work specification that's suddenly visible in places it wasn't before.

The uncomfortable part isn't learning a new skill.

It's realizing how often that skill wasn't being used—because it didn't have to be.

Until it did.

10

TARGET Is Not Audience

Clarity of intent isn't enough.

Work only starts to matter once it's aimed at someone who can actually do something with it.

That distinction sounds small. It isn't.

Most of the time, when work lands wrong, the failure isn't that people didn't understand it. It's that it reached people who couldn't act on it—and never reached the people who could.

The report goes to the stakeholders who wanted visibility. The decision sits with someone else.

The update goes to the entire team. The person who needs to execute gets the same version as everyone who's just staying informed.

The summary is clear, thorough, and accurate. And the person reading it has no authority to do anything with what's in it.

Nothing about the work itself is broken.

The problem is where it landed.

That's what TARGET controls in WTF. Not who reads the work. Who carries responsibility for what happens next.

This came up constantly in my own work, usually in ways I didn't notice until later.

I'd send something to the person who asked for it. Clear. Complete. On time. And then nothing would happen.

Not because they disagreed. Not because the work was wrong. But because they weren't the one who could move it forward. They were staying informed. Someone else—someone I hadn't thought to include—was the one who actually had to decide or act.

The work was aimed at the wrong person. And because of that, it sat.

This isn't about forgetting to cc someone.

It's about misunderstanding what role the work needed to play in someone's day.

Some people need work so they can make a decision.

Some people need it so they can execute a decision someone else already made.

Some people need it to understand what's happening, without doing anything directly.

Those are not the same TARGET.

And when work is shaped for one but sent to another, it doesn't just feel off. It stops moving.

A plan built for an executor won't help a decision-maker choose between options. It will feel too detailed, too certain, too far down the path.

A summary built for a decision-maker won't help an executor do the work. It will feel too high-level, too vague about the mechanics.

The work itself might be solid. But when it's aimed wrong, it creates friction instead of forward motion.

What makes this harder to spot is that the person receiving it will often try to make it work anyway.

They'll extract what they need. Fill in what's missing. Adjust it to fit their role. And because they're capable, it usually works—but it costs time, and the work still didn't land cleanly.

That adjustment is invisible most of the time.

You don't see it happen. You just notice that things took longer than they should have, or that follow-up questions came back, or that the output sat unused.

By then, it's hard to trace it back to TARGET. It just feels like normal work friction.

Work aimed at people who need to stay informed doesn't help people who need to decide.

Work aimed at reviewers doesn't help owners.

Work aimed at the person who asked for it doesn't always reach the person who's responsible for what comes next.

That last one shows up constantly.

Someone requests work. That person becomes the assumed TARGET. And the actual person who needs it—the one with decision authority, execution responsibility, or budget control—never sees it shaped for them.

The result is correct.

It's just aimed at the wrong part of the system.

TARGET is the part of WTF that determines whether anything actually happens after the work is done.

Not whether people understood it.

Not whether it was received.

Whether it reached someone positioned to move it forward—and was shaped in a way that let them do that without translating it first.

When TARGET is wrong, the work can be flawless.

It just won't go anywhere.

11

FORMAT Is Where
Consequences Show Up

The work can be correct, aimed properly, and still not work.

That sounds like a contradiction until you watch it happen a few times.

It's the last place failure tends to hide.

Someone delivers exactly what was asked for. The information is accurate. The WHAT is sound. The TARGET is correct.

And then it sits.

Not because it's wrong. Because using it would take more effort than starting over.

That's where FORMAT shows up.

Not as preference. As consequence.

The WHAT can be solid. The TARGET can be right. But if the shape of the output doesn't match how it needs to be used, the work stops moving.

No one announces that it failed. It just quietly creates friction instead of momentum.

An email with all the context arrives at the right time—and gets skimmed, then set aside. A few days later, someone replies asking for a shorter version they can actually use.

A document answers every question, but only if you read it top to bottom. Anyone trying to act on it has to extract the parts that matter first.

Meeting notes capture everything that was said, but bury the actions in paragraphs. The next person rewrites them before doing anything with them.

The content is there. The WHAT is done. The TARGET is right.

The FORMAT makes using it harder than it should be.

That's not a style problem.

It's a design problem.

FORMAT isn't about how something looks. It's about whether the person receiving it can do what they need to do without restructuring the entire thing first.

When FORMAT is wrong, the failure is quiet.

No error message. No rejection. Just workarounds.

Someone copies the useful parts into a new document. Someone rewrites the update before forwarding it. Someone rebuilds the table so they can see what actually matters.

That extra step—the one that shouldn't need to exist—is where clarity dies.

Not because the work was unclear.

Because clarity in the wrong shape is still unusable.

I kept seeing this in handoffs.

Someone would document their work thoroughly. What happened. What was decided. What needs to happen next. All the information was there.

And the next person still had to spend twenty minutes figuring out where to start.

Not because they didn't understand the work.

Because the structure of the handoff matched how it was written, not how it was going to be used.

Tasks buried in paragraphs. Decisions scattered across sections. Context that mattered later placed where it was easy to miss.

Nothing wrong.

Just shaped for the person who produced it, not the person who had to use it.

That gap shows up everywhere work moves between people or systems.

A budget breakdown is complete but organized by category when the decision needs to be made by priority.

A performance review covers everything required but doesn't make it obvious what actually needs to change.

A client deliverable answers every question, but in an order that forces them to hunt for what they care about most.

The work is done. The WHAT is complete. The TARGET is correct. The FORMAT is misaligned.

What makes this hard to fix after the fact is that reshaping something takes almost as much effort as creating it in the first place.

By the time someone realizes the FORMAT is wrong, they're already past the point where fixing it feels worth it.

So they don't.

They work around it. Or quietly replace it with something easier to use.

That's why FORMAT failures don't announce themselves.

They just slow things down in ways that are hard to trace back to a single decision.

This shows up most clearly in anything meant to support a decision.

An analysis lays out options in detail but doesn't surface the trade-offs that actually matter.

A project tracker is accurate but doesn't make it easy to see what's blocked or at risk.

A research summary includes every finding but doesn't separate what's certain from what's still unclear.

The WHAT is sound. The TARGET is right.

The FORMAT turns usable work into extra effort.

That's the part most people don't notice until it's too late.

By the time the output proves hard to use, the moment to shape it differently has passed. What's left is friction.

FORMAT is where that friction becomes real.

Not as failure.

As consequence.

When FORMAT aligns with how the work needs to be used, everything downstream gets easier.

When it doesn't, the work may still be correct—but it creates more problems than it solves.

That's not about polish. Or presentation.

It's about whether the person on the receiving end can take what you gave them and move forward without having to rebuild it first.

When they can, the work flows.

When they can't, it stops.

No one says it failed.

It just becomes something they have to fix before they can use it.

And by then, it's already too late to go back and shape it differently.

12

The Work Got Done.
The Problem Didn't.

The work got done.

Not in a questionable way. Not half-finished. Not sloppy. Done.

And sometimes that's the problem.

Because "done" usually means the task was completed. It doesn't always mean anything changed.

Once you start seeing work through WTF, that difference gets harder to ignore.

For most of our professional lives, completing the task was the measure.

You wrote the report. You sent the email. You updated the document. You delivered the analysis.

The work moved forward. Someone received it. It went into a folder, a thread, a meeting deck.

That counted as progress.

And most of the time, it was. Because the person on the receiving end could extract what they needed, fill in the gaps, and keep moving.

But there's a version of "done" that looks identical from the outside and feels completely different once you're holding it.

The task was completed. Nothing about the situation changed.

The report got written, but no decision got clearer.

The email got sent, but the confusion stayed exactly where it was.

The update got delivered, but the person reading it still didn't know what to do next.

Nothing failed. Nothing broke.

The work just stopped mattering.

Sometimes you even get a thank you.

Polite. Appreciative. End of thread.

And you're left wondering what just happened.

Not because the work was wrong — but because nothing moved. No decision. No change. No next step. Just closure without impact.

That feeling is hard to place at first.

It's not dramatic enough to call a failure. The output exists. It's professional. It covers what it was supposed to cover.

But when you go to use it, there's nothing to use it for.

It doesn't move anything forward. It doesn't resolve anything. It doesn't make the next step easier.

It just sits there. Completed.

This happens constantly.

The summary that includes every detail but doesn't help anyone see what matters.

The plan that lays out every step but doesn't help anyone decide whether to start.

The task got done. The problem didn't.

For a long time, this version of "done" was still acceptable.

Not ideal—but workable.

Because the person receiving the work could figure out what it was meant to do. They could infer the outcome. They could shape it into something useful.

They weren't better at the task. They just carried more context.

That repair happened quietly, so often, it became invisible.

The work landed incomplete, and someone else completed it—by understanding what it was supposed to accomplish.

That environment doesn't exist everywhere anymore.

When work moves through systems that don't interpret, the repair doesn't happen.

The work arrives exactly as it was sent. Complete in form. Unclear in function.

What gets exposed is how often the task was defined, but the outcome wasn't.

That's the piece that starts standing out once WTF becomes visible.

Not TARGET. Not FORMAT.

WHAT.

The question that should have been answered before anything started:
what is this supposed to accomplish once it exists?

Not what it is. What it does.

When WHAT is missing, everything else can be right and the work still won't matter.

The TARGET can be correct.
The FORMAT can be usable.
The content can be accurate.

But if the work doesn't create the outcome it needed to create—if it doesn't move a decision forward, reduce confusion, or change what someone does next—it just takes up space.

This is why WHAT ends up feeling heavier than the other two.

When TARGET is wrong, work stalls.

When FORMAT is wrong, work creates friction.

Both of those show themselves quickly. Someone asks a question. Someone pushes back. Someone says this doesn't work.

But when WHAT is missing—when the task was completed and the outcome was never defined—the failure is quieter.

The work doesn't fail.

It just doesn't help.

And because it looks done, it's easy to move on without noticing.

That's what becomes uncomfortable once you start seeing it.

Not the work that fails.

Meetings that end on time, with notes, and no one any clearer about what happens next.

None of that used to feel like a problem.

It felt like normal work. A little inefficient, maybe. But not broken.

What's different now is that inefficiency shows up immediately.

Not because people got less capable. But because the environment stopped absorbing ambiguity automatically.

When a human receives incomplete work, they can usually figure out what it was meant to do.

When a system receives incomplete work, it completes the task as defined.

If the outcome wasn't part of the task, the outcome doesn't exist.

That gap doesn't get repaired. It gets reflected back.

And once you've seen that pattern enough times, it becomes harder to ignore elsewhere.

You notice requests that describe the task clearly but never mention what the task is meant to accomplish.

Briefs that specify deliverables but not what those deliverables need to do once delivered.

Instructions that cover audience and format but leave out whether the goal is to inform, persuade, or help someone decide.

All of that used to get filled in later.

Now it just stays missing.

The task gets completed.
The output gets delivered.
The system does exactly what it was told.

And sometimes, nothing changes.

Not because the work was bad.

Because the work was aimed at finishing a task, not creating an outcome.

This is why WTF stops feeling like an AI thing.

It's not a trick. Not phrasing. Not a way to get better output.

It's what you use to notice when work is about to look finished and still won't matter.

And once that's visible, it's hard to keep treating "done" like an endpoint.

ACT III

13

Where Execution Actually Belongs

This is usually where books change tone.

The problems have been identified. The framework has been named. And now, finally, it's time to talk about doing something.

That's not what happens here.

Act III isn't about execution in the sense most people expect. It doesn't teach techniques, workflows, or ways to get better results out of tools. It doesn't show you how to move faster or be more efficient.

It exists to correct a misunderstanding.

For a long time, it was easy to believe that execution was the hard part of work. Writing the thing. Building the thing. Running the analysis. Producing the output.

Tools promised to make that easier. Faster. Less painful.

And in many cases, they did.

What they didn't change is the part of the process that actually determines whether the work matters once it's done.

Execution doesn't decide what the work is for. It doesn't decide who needs to use it. It doesn't decide what "usable" means in a given situation.

It never did.

What execution does is follow instructions faithfully. When those instructions are clear, that faithfulness is useful. When they aren't, the result still looks finished—just not aligned with what anyone needed.

That distinction is easy to miss when execution and thinking happen in the same place.

When you're doing the work yourself, you refine as you go. You notice when something feels off and adjust. The thinking happens inside the act of making.

When work moves through tools and systems, that loop breaks.

Execution becomes visible as execution. It stops compensating for unclear intent. It stops repairing what was left unstated.

That's not a flaw. It's the point.

Act III is about placing execution back where it belongs in the system.

Not as a source of intelligence. Not as a substitute for judgment. But as a mirror that reflects whatever clarity—or ambiguity—was present before the work ever started.

The chapters that follow don't show you how to execute better.

They show why execution keeps exposing things you didn't realize were missing.

And why that exposure isn't something to fix.

It's something to understand.

14

Understanding Isn't the Bottleneck

Tools promised to make execution faster. And for a while, that felt like progress.

What's become clearer over time is that execution wasn't the bottleneck people thought it was.

The bottleneck was knowing exactly what needed to be made in the first place.

Not vaguely. Not approximately. But clearly enough that someone else could execute it without having to reconstruct your entire thought process along the way.

That distinction matters more than it used to.

For most of our working lives, thinking and doing happened in the same place. You figured out what was needed while you were making it. You adjusted as you went. Execution and refinement were intertwined.

That worked because the person doing the work was also the person carrying the context.

When something didn't make sense, you paused. When a detail was missing, you filled it in. The gaps got closed in real time by the same person who created them.

Tools don't work that way.

They execute instructions. They don't reconstruct intent. They don't pause to interpret what you probably meant.

When the instruction is clear, that's useful.

When it isn't, the result reflects the ambiguity back without comment.

That isn't a limitation. It's the point.

A calculator doesn't teach you math. It performs calculations. If you know what problem you're solving, it saves time. If you don't, it gives you a precise answer to the wrong question.

The calculator isn't broken. The problem was never defined clearly enough to calculate.

The same pattern shows up wherever tools meet ambiguity.

Spellcheck doesn't make writing clear. It flags words that don't exist. If a sentence is confusing, spellcheck doesn't notice.

A GPS doesn't decide where you should go. It calculates routes based on the destination you provide. If the destination is wrong, the route will be efficient and useless.

An IDE doesn't write code. It executes logic as defined. If the logic is incomplete, the program runs and produces the wrong result. Confidently.

In every case, the tool does exactly what it's designed to do.

It executes faithfully.

What it doesn't do is think.

That part was always on you.

And that's the part most people don't realize they were skipping until the output comes back wrong.

The discomfort people feel with tools isn't about the tools themselves. It's about what the tools make visible.

When work moved from person to person, ambiguity got absorbed quietly. Someone asked a follow-up question. Someone made a judgment call. Someone filled in the blanks based on shared context.

The thinking that happened in those moments was real. It just didn't look like thinking.

Now that work moves through systems that don't absorb ambiguity, the gap between thinking and execution becomes obvious.

The output doesn't adjust for what you probably meant. It doesn't notice when something doesn't make sense. It just follows the instruction and finishes.

That exposure is uncomfortable.

Not because the tool is doing something wrong. But because it forces you to see how much thinking you assumed would happen automatically.

When someone says a tool feels unreliable, what they usually mean is that the output didn't match what they expected.

But the tool wasn't guessing. It was executing.

The instruction was incomplete, and the incompleteness only became visible once it was followed exactly.

That isn't a failure of capability.

It's a failure of finished thinking.

Tools can execute faster than you can. They can process more than you can. They can generate output at a scale you couldn't manage manually.

What they can't do is decide what the work is meant to accomplish, who it needs to serve, or what "usable" actually means in context.

That still requires judgment — not more expertise or experience.

The reason tools expose this so sharply is that they fill in missing context without knowing whether it fits.

A person might notice that your request doesn't quite make sense and ask a clarifying question. They might adjust based on what seems reasonable.

A tool does none of that.

It takes the instruction as given and moves forward. If something is missing, it resolves the gap without asking.

That faithfulness is what makes tools useful. It's also what makes them feel unpredictable when the thinking wasn't finished.

The tool isn't failing.

It's reflecting.

Once that becomes clear, the reaction to tools shifts.

They stop feeling like replacements and start feeling like execution surfaces.

They don't think for you. They make your thinking visible by following it exactly.

When the thinking is clear, the output is useful.

When it isn't, the output shows you where the gaps are.

That feedback used to take longer to surface. You'd hand something off, wait for questions, realize what was missing, and clarify.

Now it happens immediately.

The speed doesn't make the work easier.

It just makes unfinished thinking harder to ignore.

And that's the shift most people are still adjusting to.

For years, execution felt like the hard part because it was slow and manual.

Tools changed that.

What they didn't change is the part that actually determines whether the work succeeds or fails.

That part was always thinking.

Tools just stopped hiding it.

15

Why Execution Exposes
Weak Thinking

Tools don't fail loudly. They fail faithfully.

When something goes wrong with AI, it's easy to assume the system made a mistake. That it misunderstood. That it invented something. Or that the technology just isn't quite ready yet.

Sometimes that's true. These systems are still evolving.

But most of the failures people experience don't come from immaturity.

They come from something else entirely.

The tool did exactly what it was told to do.

Not what you meant. Not what you hoped for. Not what made sense in context.

What you specified.

The gap between those two things is where most failures live.

When an instruction leaves something unstated, execution doesn't pause to ask for clarification. It moves forward with whatever interpretation fits the pattern. That interpretation is reasonable. Defensible. Sometimes even correct in a narrow sense.

It's just not the one you had in mind.

That's the part that makes these failures so disorienting.

The output doesn't look broken. It follows the instruction. It sounds confident. It checks the obvious boxes.

What it reveals is that the instruction itself had room for interpretation you didn't realize was there.

Execution makes that visible.

Not because the system is being careless or adversarial. Quite the opposite. It's trying to comply. It's doing exactly what it was built to do — produce something that fits the instruction it was given.

This is why near-miss failures are so common.

The result is almost right. Ninety percent there. Close enough that it looks like it should work.

But that last ten percent matters. And the system had no way of knowing which ten percent to prioritize, because that part was never said.

So it made a choice. A reasonable one. Just not yours.

What makes this harder to catch is how well the output reads.

It sounds polished. Coherent. Complete.

That smoothness makes it easy to assume the thinking behind it is solid too. You skim instead of verify. You move forward instead of pausing to ask whether it actually does what it needs to do.

That's when the problem shows up—later, when the work meets reality and reality cares about the details that were never specified.

The frustration comes from the fact that nothing looks obviously wrong in the moment.

You asked for a summary. You got a summary.

You asked for an explanation. You got an explanation.

You asked for a plan. You got a plan.

The issue isn't that the tool ignored the instruction. It's that the instruction left critical decisions unstated, and execution forced those decisions to be made anyway.

Without input, the system filled in the blanks. It completed the pattern using whatever seemed most reasonable.

Humans do this too.

A decision made without upstream context can be technically correct and still derail everything downstream. The choice isn't wrong in isolation — it's wrong for the situation it was meant to serve.

What people often miss is that this isn't unique to AI.

Weak thinking has always existed. Humans are just better at compensating for it.

When you hand off incomplete work to another person, they notice the gaps. They ask questions.

They push back. Or they make assumptions informed by context and experience.

That tolerance made ambiguity survivable.

Execution without interpretation doesn't have that tolerance.

It takes the instruction as given and runs with it. If something is missing, it resolves the gap and moves on.

The result reflects the instruction exactly. Every omission. Every unstated assumption. Every place where clarity should have been and wasn't.

That's why these failures feel personal.

And once you understand WTF, they tend to feel even more so — because you can see exactly where the thinking stopped.

It's not that the tool broke your work.

It's that it showed you where your thinking stopped being complete.

And that revelation is uncomfortable.

Not because it means you did something wrong. But because it makes visible the places where you skipped steps you didn't realize you were skipping.

The parts you assumed would be obvious. The decisions you thought didn't need to be spelled out. The context you carried in your head and never actually communicated.

Execution didn't create those gaps.

It just stopped covering for them.

That's also why looking for better wording rarely solves the problem.

You can rephrase the same incomplete instruction over and over and still get drift. Different drift, maybe. But drift nonetheless.

Because the missing piece isn't in how it was said.

It's in what was never said at all.

Execution exposes that immediately. Consistently. Without commentary or correction.

And once you see that pattern, it becomes harder to blame the tool for doing exactly what it was designed to do.

The discomfort doesn't come from execution failing.

It comes from realizing the instruction was weaker than it felt while you were writing it.

Execution didn't break the work.

It revealed what was missing.

16

Where This Breaks at Scale

Ambiguity doesn't disappear as work scales.

It multiplies.

What feels manageable when it's just you—a vague instruction here, an unstated assumption there—becomes something else when that same work moves through multiple people, across teams, through systems that don't repair misunderstandings in real time.

At small scale, ambiguity gets absorbed. Someone asks a question. Someone fills in a gap. The work adjusts as it moves forward.

That stops working somewhere between three and five handoffs.

Not because people stop caring. Not because anyone becomes careless.

But because each person in the chain inherits not just the work, but every unstated assumption that came before it.

By the time something reaches the third or fourth person, no one is working from the original intent anymore. They're working from the last interpretation, which was itself shaped by the interpretation before that.

The gaps don't close.

They propagate.

A team gets a request to "improve onboarding." No one defines what improvement means in this case. Faster. Simpler. Different users. Different outcomes.

Each handoff adds detail without resolving that question.

By the time the work ships, it's complete. It does what the brief said. But it doesn't solve the problem that started the work.

No one failed. No one ignored instructions.

The work just drifted—one reasonable interpretation at a time—until it arrived somewhere no one intended.

That's what happens when unstated intent moves through a system.

It doesn't stay unstated. It gets filled in by whoever touched it last.

And once it's filled in, it looks like it was always part of the plan.

The other thing that happens at scale is that accountability fractures.

When work stays with one person, they own the outcome. If something isn't clear, they notice. If a decision needs to be made, they make it or escalate it.

When work moves across teams, ownership becomes diffuse.

The person who wrote the request assumes the next person will ask if something is unclear.

The next person assumes the details were already settled upstream.

The person after that assumes the hard decisions were made somewhere else.

No one is avoiding responsibility. Everyone is doing their job.

But the work is moving through a structure where each person believes someone else has it.

And the thing no one actually has is clarity.

When a system is built on unstated assumptions, the failures don't just miss the mark.

They miss in ways that are hard to trace back to a single decision, a single person, or a single moment.

That's how responsibility becomes blurry. That's how fixes turn into blame. Not because someone caused the problem—but because no one can clearly point to where it entered the system.

This is where WTF stops being about individual skill and starts being about infrastructure.

When one person is unclear, the result is frustrating but fixable.

When a system is built on unstated assumptions, the failures don't just miss the mark. They miss structurally.

The gaps aren't isolated.

They're embedded.

A strategy gets defined at the top. It's high-level by design.

That becomes input for the next layer down. They interpret it. Add detail. Make choices.

Their output becomes input for the next group. Who do the same.

By the time the work reaches the people executing it, it's an interpretation of an interpretation of an interpretation.

At that point, questioning it doesn't feel like clarification.

It feels like starting over.

Or worse, like admitting ignorance—something most people try to avoid once work has momentum.

So the work moves forward.

That reveals why the phrase "let's just get it done" is so common, especially in large organizations.

Not because people don't care about quality. But because reopening clarity after several handoffs feels more expensive than pushing through and hoping it works.

So the work keeps moving.

And the gaps keep compounding.

What makes this especially difficult to address is that most of the time, nothing looks obviously broken.

The handoffs happen. The meetings occur. The documentation exists.

The problem shows up later—in the outcome, or in the absence of the outcome anyone actually wanted.

There's another pattern that only becomes visible at scale.

Clarity decays faster than ambiguity.

When something is explicit, it has to survive every handoff intact. When it gets summarized or cleaned up, details drop out.

Ambiguity survives more easily. It moves forward without resistance because it doesn't make claims that can be challenged.

A clear instruction can be questioned.

An ambiguous one just gets interpreted.

Over time, systems favor what causes the least friction in the moment.

And ambiguity causes less friction than clarity.

Right up until the work is done and no one can use it.

What's striking about this pattern is how predictable it is.

If you trace a failure backward far enough, you almost always find the same thing.

Somewhere near the beginning, someone assumed something was obvious.

That assumption moved forward as if it were fact.

By the time it reached the people executing the work, it had been reinforced enough that questioning it would have felt like starting over.

So no one questioned it.

And the system amplified what it was given.

Individual clarity doesn't solve this.

One precise person doesn't stop the next three interpretations from stripping away specificity.

At scale, WTF isn't a personal habit.

It's infrastructure.

Either it's built into how work moves—or it isn't.

And when it isn't, the gaps don't stay small.

They become the system.

17

Seniority, Experience, and the Myth of Intuition

Experience didn't remove ambiguity.

It absorbed it.

When someone with years in a role gets handed something incomplete, they don't stop to ask what was left out. They fill it in. They know what usually matters. They know where things tend to break. They know which questions need answers before something becomes a problem.

That isn't magic.

It's pattern recognition built over time.

They've seen enough versions of the same situation to recognize what's missing. They've fixed enough mistakes to know which details actually matter. They've worked in the system long enough to infer intent even when it isn't stated clearly.

That ability to fill gaps quietly is what made experience valuable.

Not just knowing how to do the work. Knowing what the work actually required when the instruction didn't spell it out.

For a long time, that worked.

If something arrived incomplete, the experienced person corrected for it. If context was missing, they added it back in. If priorities weren't stated, they inferred them based on everything else they knew.

Most of the time, they got it right.

And when they didn't, the failure surfaced early enough to be fixed. Someone noticed. Someone pushed back. Someone clarified.

The ambiguity never went away.

It just got absorbed by people who had enough context to handle it without slowing things down.

That created a quiet dependency.

The system didn't require clarity because experienced people compensated for its absence. Instructions could stay vague because someone downstream would figure out what was actually needed. Handoffs could leave things unstated because the next person had seen it before.

It looked like efficiency.

It felt like trust.

What it actually was: a repair mechanism running in the background, invisible until it stopped working.

That mechanism had limits.

It scaled as long as the same people stayed in the loop. As long as the experienced person could see the work, touch it, correct it before it drifted too far.

When that became harder, systems adapted.

Organizations created buffer roles. Layers whose job was to catch what wasn't specified. People were groomed to hold context so the system wouldn't collapse.

That wasn't accidental.

Patching the system was easier than fixing the root cause — especially when it wasn't clear that anything was missing in the first place.

There was another side effect too.

Over time, unspoken knowledge became a form of stability. Context lived in people. That created continuity, and often job security. A pattern that made sense in the environment it emerged from, and one that's difficult to unwind.

The problem isn't the people who carried that knowledge.

The system was built to rely on it.

But the moment work moved outside that loop — to someone new, to a different team, to systems without the same context — the gaps reappeared.

Suddenly the instruction that worked fine internally didn't work anymore. The handoff that felt obvious to people who'd been around for years confused everyone else.

Nothing about the instruction had changed.

What changed was who received it.

When experience was present, the ambiguity got absorbed.

When it wasn't, it didn't.

That's where the scaling problem shows up.

Not because junior people are less capable. But because they're being asked to do something experience makes invisible — fill in context that was never communicated.

That isn't a skill you can train directly.

You can't teach someone to infer what wasn't said. You can't shortcut pattern recognition that takes years to develop.

What you can do is stop depending on it.

The alternative isn't removing experienced people from the process.

It's making what they carry explicit enough that it doesn't have to live inside them.

That shift feels unnatural at first.

If you've spent years reading between the lines, spelling everything out can feel like overkill. Like you're explaining things that should be obvious.

They feel obvious because you already have the context.

The person on the other end doesn't. And neither does the system the work now passes through.

This is what WTF makes visible.

Not the work itself — the assumptions experienced people carry so automatically they no longer recognize them as assumptions.

WHAT the work is supposed to accomplish.
TARGET who it actually needs to serve.
FORMAT what "usable" looks like when it's finished.

Experienced people internalize these so deeply they don't think about them consciously anymore.

And that's exactly why the knowledge is hard to transfer.

When asked how they knew to do something a certain way, the answer is often some version of "I just knew." Or "It made sense in the situation."

Both are true.

Neither helps someone who doesn't have the same history.

What used to be absorbed by experience now has to be made explicit.

Not because experience stopped mattering.

But because the assumption that experience will always be in the loop no longer holds.

Work moves faster. It touches more people. It passes through systems that don't interpret the way humans do.

The repair mechanism that used to catch things quietly can't keep up anymore.

That doesn't make intuition useless.

It means intuition alone can't carry the system.

The judgment of experienced people still matters. It just can't stay locked inside them if the work is expected to function without constant correction.

This isn't about flattening hierarchies or reducing the role of senior people.

It's about recognizing that relying on their ability to absorb ambiguity hid a structural gap that was always there.

WTF externalizes what used to live in people.

It doesn't replace judgment.

It makes it transferable.

That shift isn't comfortable.

But once you see it, it's hard to ignore.

Not because things suddenly work better.

But because it becomes obvious how much work was functioning only because someone else was quietly fixing what was never specified.

18

What Changes Once You Can't Unsee This

Nothing dramatic changed.

You're still asking for the same kinds of work. Still writing emails, making decisions, handing things off to other people. The tools might be different. The process looks mostly the same.

But something shifted anyway.

It's subtle at first. You catch yourself before hitting send. You notice a sentence that assumes too much and rewrite it without thinking about it. You read someone else's request and immediately see what's missing—not because they did anything wrong, but because the shape is now obvious.

That recognition doesn't feel like a skill you learned.

Like when someone points out that arrows are hidden in the FedEx logo, or that most people breathe irregularly, or that your tongue never quite rests comfortably in your mouth. Once it's been named, it's just there. You don't have to look for it.

WTF works the same way.

At some point, you stop consciously checking whether the work specifies what it's supposed to accomplish, who it's for, or what "usable" means. You just notice when one of those pieces is missing.

Not because you're trying to.

Because the gap is now visible in a way it wasn't before.

That isn't always comfortable. And that's a good thing.

It means noticing how often things were left unstated. How much work moved forward on assumptions that never got checked. How many decisions were made based on outputs that looked fine but weren't actually complete.

And once you see it in your own work, you start seeing it everywhere else.

In meetings that drift because no one defined what decision needed to be made.

In documents that check every box but don't help anyone do anything.

In handoffs that assume the next person will figure out what matters.

None of this makes those situations easier to fix. Sometimes they still happen the same way. Sometimes the environment doesn't support the kind of clarity that would actually help.

But the difference is that you're no longer confused about why things went wrong.

The failure doesn't feel random.

It feels predictable.

And predictability, even when the outcome isn't great, removes the surprise.

That's the shift.

Not that everything suddenly works better. Not that AI is now perfect. Not that ambiguity stopped being part of how work gets done.

Just that when something lands wrong, you can see what was missing.

And when something lands right, you can see why.

The strangest part is how quickly it stops feeling like a framework.

WTF was useful at first because it gave the pattern a name. It made vague frustration easier to talk about. It turned something fuzzy into something visible.

But after a while, you stop referencing it consciously.

You don't think in terms of steps or checks. You just notice the shape of what's missing and adjust without thinking about it.

It becomes part of how you see work.

Not something you apply.

Something you notice.

That's when it becomes permanent.

You can ignore it. You can decide not to act on it. But you can't go back to not seeing it.

This isn't empowerment. It isn't a new capability.

It's just a shift in what draws your attention.

And what draws your attention changes everything else downstream.

Not because you're trying to work differently.

Because the lens changed.

Some of that makes work smoother. Some of it makes work more frustrating, because you're now seeing gaps that no one else is noticing or that no one has time to close.

Both can be true at the same time.

What doesn't change is that clarity still matters.

It mattered before AI. It mattered when work moved between people who could ask follow-up questions and adjust in real time. It mattered when being vague was safe because the environment absorbed ambiguity.

It just matters more now.

Not because the standard went up.

Because the buffer went away.

When something is unclear, it doesn't get softened or corrected downstream. It moves forward as-is. And whatever was missing stays missing until someone notices and loops back.

That loop costs time. It creates friction. It makes work feel unreliable even when everyone involved is competent and trying.

WTF doesn't fix that.

But it makes the cause easier to see.

And once the cause is visible, the rest becomes easier to navigate—not because the problems disappeared, but because they're no longer surprising.

That's all this was ever about.

Not making AI smarter. Not making you faster. Not unlocking a new way of working that changes everything.

Just seeing what was already there.

What's been shaping outcomes quietly for as long as work has moved from intention to execution.

AI didn't create that gap.

It just made it impossible to ignore.

And now that you've seen it, it doesn't go away.

You'll notice it tomorrow. In a request that assumes too much. In an output that looks right but doesn't help. In a conversation that drifts because the purpose was never clear.

Not because you're looking for it.

Because it's there.

And once you see it,

you just do.

Epilogue

Nothing in this book asked you to change how you work.

It didn't offer techniques. It didn't give you steps to follow. It didn't promise better outcomes if you applied anything correctly.

That was intentional.

Because nothing here was new.

The gap between intention and execution has always existed. Work has always depended on what was stated, what was assumed, and what was left unsaid. For most of our working lives, that gap stayed mostly invisible—not because it wasn't there, but because people filled it in without being asked.

AI didn't create the gap.

It just stopped covering for it.

What this book did was make that visible. Not as a flaw. Not as a failure. Just as a structural reality that's been shaping outcomes quietly for a long time.

You don't "use" this perspective. You don't apply it like a technique. It just changes what you notice.

You see when work is defined by tasks instead of outcomes.
WHAT

You see when something is aimed at the wrong place in the system.
TARGET

You see when an output looks complete but won't actually be usable.
FORMAT

You also see why none of that feels dramatic in the moment.

Work still moves. Outputs still get produced. Everything looks reasonable—right up until the moment it doesn't.

That's not a new problem.

It's just harder to ignore now.

This book doesn't resolve that tension. It doesn't tell you how to eliminate it. It only makes it clear why it exists, and why it shows up the way it does.

Once that's clear, the tension doesn't disappear..

And once you've seen it, it doesn't go away.

About the Author

Andres has spent his career working at the intersection of systems, technology, and the people expected to make sense of both. While much of that work predates AI, the same patterns have become harder to ignore as AI systems entered real execution paths—where assumptions are no longer absorbed quietly and intent has to survive being specified.

www.ingramcontent.com/pod-product-compliance
Lightning Source LLC
Chambersburg PA
CBHW071601200326
41519CB00021BB/6825